Dr. Millard B. Box

INSPIRATION
OF THE
SCRIPTURES

2 Timothy 3:16

LAURUS BOOKS

INSPIRATION

OF THE

SCRIPTURES

Dr. Millard B. Box

Paperback: ISBN: 978-1-938526-98-5

Mobi (Kindle): ISBN: 978-1-938526-99-2

Published by LAURUS BOOKS

LAURUS BOOKS
P.O. Box 530173
DeBary, FL 32753-0173 USA
www.TheLaurusCompany.com

This book may be purchased in paperback from TheLaurusCompany.com, Amazon.com, and other retailers around the world. Also available in formats for electronic readers from their respective stores.

INSPIRATION

OF THE

SCRIPTURES

All Scripture is given by inspiration of God,
and is profitable for doctrine, for reproof,
for correction, for instruction in righteousness.

2 Timothy 3:16

Dedication

This book is dedicated to

Stephen B. Box

my son,
who, at the time of this writing,
was just starting the pathway of
preaching His Word. May he
forever believe and preach the
Word without presuming to
sit in judgment on God's
infallible text.

Preface

Although this message was first delivered several years ago from the time of this release, the content is needed as much if not more today as when it was delivered to the Baptist Pastor's Conference in Houston. The heresies that are creeping into the church today are equally as evil as those from outside the church.

I am very grateful to those who have been my teachers in the past years, those who started me out in the ministry believing the Word of God to *be* the Word of God. I praise the Lord for a believing heart, rather than a suspicious mind.

I submit this writing to those who desire to be encouraged in believing the Word, and especially to the young preachers, so that they might be grounded in the truth that God speaks without error in His Word.

—Millard B. Box

INTRODUCTION

Introduction

1 Corinthians 2:1-14

In the midst of a world gone mad, I heard someone ask, "Why does God not speak?" Our answer to that question is, "God *has* spoken." He has spoken in the natural and the supernatural. He has spoken in His Son. God's Son is the Living Word.

> *God, who at sundry times and in divers manners spake in time past unto the fathers by the prophets, hath in these last days spoken unto us by His Son ...* (Hebrews 1:1-2)

There is a world of difference between knowing the Word of God and the God of the Word. I am urged to say that it is impossible to know the written Word unless you know, first of all, the Living Word. God has spoken by the written Word, as well as by His Living Word, Jesus Christ.

However, in the midst of this reeling world that is staggering economically, physically, and religiously into utter chaos, we find subtle Satan sowing seeds of doubt and characteristically planting question marks on the authenticity of His written Word! The scientific world has now broken the space barrier; the lustful world has broken the sin barrier; but, please God, someone needs to break the doubt barrier as to His divinely ascribed Word. God, raise up that man or those men.

The Bible—God's Holy Word, Scripture—is the very keel of the ship of Christianity. If the waves of worldliness engulf it, then there is no hope. God's Word is the Keystone in the arch of Truth. If modern doubt is able to destroy that Keystone, then there is no place for the door of salvation. God's Word is the foundation of Faith. If we do not build on that, then the tides of higher criticism, so-called, will sweep away our house of Faith.

It seems that all the forces of the foes of Christianity are massed against the Word of God today. If these worldwide, Satan-inspired forces can undermine our confidence in the Word; if its inerrant, infallible inspiration can be made a fable; if our leaders today in their so-called modern thinking (which is not very modern, nor with much thought, either) can assassinate with their penknife of rationalism and cut out the heart of the Word (see Jeremiah 36:23); if all this can be done, I say if, then God help us in both this and in future generations.

Now, may I give you a few thoughts as a word of testimony that we might begin to love what is given us by the Lord? I come not as a braggart nor with the spirit of a know-it-all. I want to tell you the conclusion I have reached after college, seminary, and other study. I take my stand here! I do not propose to change your thought if you do not agree. I merely wish for us to pitch our mental tents on these grounds for a while. If you agree, fine. If you disagree, I will still love you in our Lord. You cannot stop me from loving you.

There are essentially three attitudes with which men regard the Word of God:

1. The first attitude is that the Bible contains a record of the history and religious thoughts of men; it consists simply of the conclusions and opinions that men have formulated as a result of life and experience.

   This attitude demands that it be treated with suspicion and that it be subject to correction on the basis of new information.

2. The second attitude is that the Bible contains *some* of the revealed truth of God, but many other things in the Bible are the result of human error and ignorance.

This attitude achieves some permanent definition of doctrine upon the repetition of those doctrines. These doctrines comprise the revelation of God and must be carefully separated from the rest of the Bible.

3. The third attitude is that the Bible, in its entirety, word for word, as written in the original manuscripts and insofar as faithfully preserved and translated, is the complete, inerrant, and exclusive revelation of God to man.

    This attitude can result in conviction of man's sinful nature, which can lead to repentance and restoration by acceptance of salvation through Jesus Christ and the infilling of His Spirit. It can bring a commitment to Truth and a life of obedience that is pleasing to God, a life of denying self, taking up one's own cross daily, and following after Jesus (Luke 9:23).

I

THINK OF HIS WORD

And His Name

1

And His Name

Higher than His creation and His re-creation (the born-again soul of man), higher than even His Name is His Word! Above all other things created by Him, God has given first place to His Word!

> *"I will worship toward Your holy temple, and praise Your name for Your loving-kindness and for Your truth* and *faithfulness; for You have exalted above all else Your name and Your word* AND *YOU HAVE MAGNIFIED YOUR WORD ABOVE ALL YOUR NAME!"*
>
> (Psalm 138:2 AMP. Emphasis added.)

Even among sinful men, a man's name is no better than his word. If God's Word is

19

derelict, then God must be derelict. Those who tamper with His Word need to realize that they are tampering with His Name. How exceedingly dangerous! How desperately foolish!

> *"And [Jesus] said to them, O foolish ones [sluggish in mind, dull of perception] and slow of heart to believe (adhere to and trust in and rely on) EVERYTHING [ALL] that the prophets have spoken! … Then beginning with Moses and [throughout] ALL the Prophets, He went on explaining and interpreting to them in ALL the Scriptures the things concerning and referring to Himself.*
>
> (Luke 24:25, 27 AMP. Emphasis added.)

Jesus was jealous for His Father's Name. His Word must be fulfilled in order that His Father's Name might be honored. Modern skepticism, rationalism, intellectualism, and theological juggling of truth bring a blight upon God by questioning His Word. Questioning His Word brings dishonor to

His Name. In Luke 1:70, Zacharias prophesied, *"As he [God] spake by the mouth of his holy prophets, which have been since the world began."*

His Name and His Word are inseparable forever!

II

THINK OF HIS WORD
And His Spirit

II

And His Spirit

Recall with me that Jesus said in John 16:13: *"... when He the spirit of truth is come, he will guide you into all truth ..."* Jesus continues in John 17:17 by saying, *"... thy word is truth."*

There are two or three thoughts I would share with you here.

1. If God is a God of Truth, then I am firmly convinced that He did not need, nor does He need, myths and legends as vehicles to tell the truth. Myths and legends are of necessity, at the very best, half-truths. Since when does a perfect God telling perfect truth rely on man-made half-

25

truths to give us perfect truth? It is not only impossible but utterly asinine to believe such a thing. Second Peter 1:21 should settle this matter for us.

For no prophecy ever originated because some man willed it [to do so—it never came by human impulse], but men spoke from God who were borne along (moved and impelled) by the Holy Spirit. (2 Peter 1:21 AMP)

2. If you will carefully study 1 Corinthians 2, you will instantly see that Scripture is not psychologically or intellectually discerned but is spiritually discerned.

But the natural, NONSPIRITUAL man does not accept or welcome or admit into his heart the gifts and teachings and revelations of the Spirit of God, for they are folly (meaningless nonsense) to him; and HE IS INCAPABLE OF KNOWING THEM ... BECAUSE THEY ARE SPIRITUALLY DISCERNED and estimated and appreciated.
(1 Corinthians 2:14 AMP. Emphasis added.)

The Bible is a strange Book. You do not understand it in order to believe it, but you must believe it in order to understand it. Frankly, the Word of God states nowhere that it is to be explained but that it is to be believed and obeyed.

Knowing Hebrew and Greek and reading the Word in the original languages does not establish a man as a master of the Word of God any more than knowing how to mix paint establishes a man as a master artist.

Unless the professor or minister is dominated and *led by* the Holy Spirit and *led of* the Holy Spirit and *filled with* the Holy Spirit, there is no assurance whatever that he is giving the right interpretation to any Scripture. If he depends on or relies on academic and theoretical knowledge rather than on the leadership of the Holy Spirit, he is depending on false foundations. Without the Holy Spirit guiding us in

Scripture belief and interpretation, our schools and our pulpits are nothing but religious laboratories where we dissect doctrine, develop dogma, and parrot professional mouthings of men of letters. By this we may well enlighten the minds of our hearers, but we do not enliven their souls. Much is being said of Academic freedom. Well might we cry for Spirit-freedom!

3. This one additional thought could well be taken from 2 Corinthians 3:6 where it states: "... *the letter killeth, but the spirit giveth life* ..." God help us to keep this in mind. We should search the Scriptures, for Jesus said in John 5:39: "*Search the scriptures; for in them ye think ye have eternal life: and they are they which testify of me.*" This He said of the Old Testament, of course. The Word of God is a sealed Book to the unsaved and to the one who

doubts it. All they see are wars. laws, exploits, songs. poems, tragedies, history, people, etc. But those who believe it see in it the Lord Jesus Christ from Genesis 1:1 to Revelation 22:21. This is the work of the Holy Spirit.

4. *Of which salvation the prophets have enquired and searched diligently, who prophesied of the grace that should come unto you: Searching what, or what manner of time the Spirit of Christ which was in them did signify, when it testified beforehand the sufferings of Christ, and the glory that should follow. Unto whom it was revealed, that not unto themselves, but unto us they did minister the things, which are now reported unto you by them that have preached the gospel unto you with the Holy Ghost sent down from heaven; which things the angels desire to look into.*

(1 Peter 1:10-12)

These Scriptures indicate four points that appertain to the Inspired Word being given to the writers:

(a) The Old Testament prophets wrote exactly what the Holy Spirit testified to them.

(b) The Old Testament prophets did not understand what they wrote. This is evidence therefore that the very words had to be given them by the Holy Spirit.

(c) The Old Testament prophets tried to understand what they had written. This is, again, evidence of the over-seership of the Holy Spirit.

(e) The Old Testament prophets wrote especially for later generations to read and believe.

III

THINK OF HIS WORD

And His Truth

III

And His Truth

I have already mentioned His Word as Truth. I did that for emphasis' sake, as to the work of the Holy Spirit. Now I wish to emphasize His Word as Truth itself in the very Words written in the original languages.

In the first Article given to the Baptist Convention in Kansas City, the words read like this. "The Holy Bible was written by men divinely inspired and is the record of God's revelation of Himself to man. It is a perfect treasure of divine instruction. It has God for its Author, salvation for its end, and truth without any mixture of error for its matter…"

The word "inspired" means "God-breathed." The word "logos," as you may

33

know, means literally "to pick out (or) select, to pick words in order to express thought." Thus, it means "to speak."

Therefore, I believe that the Word of God is verbally inspired in the original languages.

The popular theory is this: "God gave the thoughts, and man clothed them in his own language." **This I do not believe!** Before you chastise or castigate me, permit me to give you some thoughts, lovingly and kindly.

1. I believe that God, perfect and divine, Truth Himself, so controlled the sacred writers in what they wrote that not only the thoughts but even the expression of those thoughts were of God to such an extent that, in the original copies, the language expresses the thought God intended to convey with such infallible accuracy that the words as well as the thoughts are God's revelation to us.

We read in 2 Timothy 3:16-17: "*ALL*

scripture is given by inspiration of God and is *profitable ...*" Not every other chapter, not every other sentence, not every other word or every tenth word, but *all* Scripture.

One theologian whose name I recall as being Dr. Brooks stated: "In the early church ... there was entire unanimity among those who had a right to be called Christians, as to inspiration itself, an inspiration that was supernatural in its source, unerring in its truthfulness, and extending to the very words of Scripture."

Origen, a theologian and prolific Biblical scholar and considered to be the greatest by far among the ante-Nicene writers, declared, "The sacred books are not the writings of men but have been written and delivered to us from the inspiration of the Holy Spirit by the will of the Father of all things, through Jesus Christ."

2. I believe the inspiration of the Scriptures extends to the words as well as the thoughts for the following reasons:

   a. Full verbal inspiration was not to secure the infallible correctness of the personal opinions of the sacred writers but to secure an infallible record of the Truth. And, a record consists of a language!

   b. Men think in words. The more definitely you think, the more definitely are your thoughts expressed with an exact verbal expression. Infallibility of thought cannot be secured, noted, or preserved without an infallible rendering. No words – no record!

      If the Bible is a mixture of truth and error, then we ourselves will have to attempt to decide what part is of God and what part is of man. Since we are fallen men, I ask you, which one of us, professor or preacher, is capable of analyzing and dissecting God's Word on purely subjective impressions or feelings, or on the basis of historical knowledge? If we do, we thereby sit in judgment on God and decide which statement from His Word is to be believed or disbelieved. We, the aliens from the life of God in consequence of the ignorance that dwells in them sitting in judgment on God's Word? How utterly unthinkable!

Without belief in the fully inerrant, infallible Word of God, rationalism mounts the throne, and our imperfect human understanding, darkened by the Fall, stands as judge over God's Book and God's Word! The accused sinner can never take the place of the Judge and decide what God may or may not have said. This applies to every jot and tittle of the Old Testament writings and to the parsing of every Greek verb in the New.

The Word must be regarded as the body of the thought. If the word is blurred, so is the thought, and all the Bible becomes indistinct. Without inspiration of its words, the thoughts of the Word would be without form. A variation of words always includes a more or less definite change in the thoughts.

Luther said, "Christ did not say of His thoughts but of His Words, 'they are spirit, and they are life'."

Spurgeon said, "We contend for every word of the Bible and believe in the verbal, literal inspiration of the Holy Scripture. Indeed, we believe there can be no other kind of inspiration. If the words are taken from us, the exact meaning is of itself lost."

We do not speak of a stiff, mechanical, dictated inspiration of the Word. The holy writers were not passive mediums but active men of God; not deed tools but living, sanctified co-workers; not slaves but friends of God.

Inspiration is not mechanical but organic; not magical but natural, not lifeless but living. Only in this way did God's Word meet us in the garment of the human languages of Hebrew, Aramaic, and Greek. But, we believe, the personal errors and failures of the human instruments were not incorporated into the personal text of what they wrote. God mysteriously filled the active human spirits of the Biblical writers and so guided and overruled them that there arose an infallible, Spirit-wrought sacred writing and record with which the Holy Spirit organically unites Himself to this very hour.

Paul said in 1 Corinthians 2:13, *"Which things also we speak, not in the words which man's wisdom teacheth, but* [the words] *which the Holy Ghost teacheth; comparing spiritual things with spiritual."*

Now hear Paul in 1 Thessalonians 2:13, *"... thank we God without ceasing, because, when ye received the word of God which ye heard of us, ye received it not as the word of men, but as it is in truth, the word of God..."*

If there is any possibility for error in words, then there must be possibility for error in thought and therefore error in writing and error in doctrine, and we are in error today.

Another theologian, Dr. Bishop, stated it well when he said, "Verbal and direct inspiration is, therefore, the Thermopylae of Biblical and Scriptural faith: no breath, no syllable; no syllable, no word; no word, no book; no book, no religion."

c. New Testament writers, when quoting the Old Testament for purposes of proving a point, often based their arguments upon the very words used. In this, they ascribed authority to word as well as thought.

Jesus quoted God word for word when He answered the Pharisees in Matthew 22:32, and as to the resurrection, He referred to Exodus 3:6: *"Moreover, He* [God] *said, I am the God of thy father, the God of Abraham, the God of Isaac, and the God of Jacob ..."*

In Matthew 22:43-44, Jesus quoted Psalm 110:1.

Paul, in Galatians 3:16, quoted the last part of Genesis 17:7.

In speaking of the first eleven chapters of Genesis, over which there has been much controversy, Paul quoted Genesis 2:2 in Hebrews 4:4. He referred to Genesis 3:16 in 1 Corinthians 14:34. And James referred to Genesis 8:21 in James 4:5.

If we are deluded for believing literally the first eleven chapters of Genesis, then, brethren, take comfort, for we are in good company. So did Paul and James.

Jesus, in John 10:34-36, quotes Psalms 82:6 and says, "... *the scripture cannot be broken ...*"

These few examples must suffice, since hours could be taken to give all the references to the Old Testament.

d. I hardly believe that Jesus would be given to erroneous statements since He is Truth even as God is Truth, and He is God. He said in Matthew 4:4: "... *Man shall not live by bread alone, but by every word that proceedeth out of the mouth of God."* He was quoting from Deuteronomy 8:3.

e. Proverbs 30:5 is plain in the statement, *"Every word of God is pure: he is a shield unto them that put their trust in Him."*

Conclusion

Conclusion

Concluding this message, I will state that I believe the Word of God, word for word, regardless of my intellectual attainment or emotional consequence. God needs neither my assertion nor denial. When I see Him face to face, I can but believe what He said as He said it. I shall not have to face Him having questioned what He said.

I believe the Word of God claims Divine authority. Its diction is by a Divine speaker; its invitation or pleadings of Divine love; its judgments are evidence of Divine righteousness; its miracles are proof of Divine power; its order is confirmation of a Divine plan; its preservation is ratification of a Divine Keeper; its spirit the declaration of a Divine Inspirer; and its wisdom is an attestation of a Divine Teacher.

Matthew Henry warned us when he said, "Satan teaches men to doubt, and then to deny. He makes them skeptics first, and so, by degrees, makes them atheists. The assault now is not only against the character of God, but also against the truth of His pronouncements."

So, brethren, receive the Word of God as His Word, verbally, inerrantly inspired. Receive it and believe it, as did the Bereans in Acts 17:11: "... *they received the Word with all readiness of mind, and searched the scriptures daily, whether those things were so.*" They received the Scriptures above the verbal testimony of an apostle ...

As servants from our Master,
As saints from the Holy One,
As subjects from the King of Kings,
As sons from the Father,
As saved souls from the Savior,
As sanctified ones from the Sanctifier.

I Trust Forever Thy Sure Promise

I trust forever thy sure promise;
Thereon the soul can safely build:
I know that not one word thou speakest
Shall fall to earth as unfilled.

The hills and mountains all may vanish,
The universe collapse and flee,
But not the smallest word thou givest,
O Lord, shall unaccomplished be!

Unknown author:

Within that awful volume lies
The mystery of mysteries:
Oh, happiest they of human race
To whom our God has granted grace.

To read, to fear, to hope, to pray.
To lift the latch, and force the way:
But better had they ne'er been born
Who read to doubt, or read to scorn.

About the Author

Dr. Millard B. Box

Dr. Millard B. Box, at 98 years young as of this release, has refused to retire. He has been preaching for 83 years, with 40 years as a Southern Baptist pastor.

Robust and healthy at his age, he is an encouraging figure to the body of Christ and a living example of the truth found in his book, *The Power of The Older Christian.*

You are sure to be touched by the wisdom and experience gained by this man from over eight decades of studying the Holy Scriptures and serving his Lord Jesus Christ.

Dr. Box travels both in the United States and in foreign countries upon invitation. He and his wife, Rachel, reside in Fairhope, Alabama.

Other books by
Dr. Millard B. Box

Invitation to Intimacy

The Power of the Older Christian

www.ingramcontent.com/pod-product-compliance
Lightning Source LLC
Chambersburg PA
CBHW071113090426
42737CB00013B/2584